"*Salt Water* is a sl genre of poetry, so candid self-help. I. ... acceptance, growth, and what it means to be human. *Salt Water* is the note you wrote to yourself years ago, which you find again when you most need it, that reminds you 'it's going to be okay.'"
—*Lee Crutchley, Author of "How To Be Happy, Or At Least Less Sad"*

"There are too many words to write and too many things to say about the power of *Salt Water*. What I can say is that I cried, made many noises of epiphanies, and felt as though I was reading the words of my soul, written down on a page. To say this book is about enlightenment would be an insult. It is the awakening of self, the seeing of light, the acceptance of darkness, and the choice for greatness just as it is right now, within each and every one of us.
—*Dionna Chambers, Spokesperson, Motivational Millennial, Creator of Dream Series TV*

"With every page I became more convinced that *Salt Water* is the book you're going to see everyone with next year. The poems are solid, simple observations that get at the universal. For anyone with questions, Wiest's poetry offers a new, wholesome perspective, a way to 'see the fractures as the design.'"
—*Chrissy Stockton, creative and partner at Thought Catalog and author of "We Are All Just A Collection Of Cords"*

"Brianna Wiest does it again. Fantastic writing of poems that are simple in nature, yet give great depth when it comes to thoughts and emotions. Loved reading each poem, as it provided something unique each time."
—*Faiz Aly, CEO of Aly Media*

SALT WATER

BRIANNA
WIEST

ISBN 978-1-945796-75-3

To S.B.

"Part of you pours out of me in these lines from time to time."

"I escape in the same mind that traps me."

—Malanda

Letting go
Is not releasing
It is allowing
What already is

I thought becoming myself
Was improving each part
Piece by piece

But it was finding
A hidden wholeness
Seeing the fractures
As the design

The universe is dyadic
Like us

Stars are not solitary
They have "companions,"
Separate, but equal planets
That keep from collapsing into one another
By opposing centrifugal force

Their distance and desire
Create the structure of the universe

Our hearts and lungs
Exist in halves
Our lives are split
By light and dark

We have sets of heart chambers
And pairs of feet
The corneas reading this
Are opposing replicas

We were born from waves and falters
We were designed to be terrified of what we want most
These forces touch
Even unconscious beams of light in the sky

But can I tell you
That what I had been looking for all that time
Was me
And there was no photo so beautiful
No dripping rose perfume
Sweat-stained towel
Dulled black cotton dress
Messy, bleached waves sticking to lip balm
Lukewarm air filling the car
Moment of stinging anxiety
That wasn't filled with the same deep knowing
I didn't fit in this world
Because I was born to help create a new one

Silence is god's language,
Simplicity is her essence

Productivity is how you run away from yourself
Creativity is how you become yourself

The things we lose are not losses

They are entryways

They are the world saying, sometimes sharply,

There is something else out there

What we are doing here is unlearning
Unbecoming everything we were taught to be
We are unlearning trends, consuming
We are undoing binds, removing pacifiers
And screaming out
We are letting go of every beautiful thing
That we thought we needed to be who we are
And discovering that we could be ourselves
Or we could be distracted
There was never anything else

You are so busy standing in your ruins
That you are not building a new city

I put the tip of my fingernail on the glass of my phone as I replay recordings of people speaking.

I feel bursts of vibration that create the word, the sound, the thought, the transmission of information. The movement of creation on my fingertip. This is how it is to realize that everything we do and are is just another formation of these tiny movements, like notes in a song. This is how it is to realize that in everything we do, we are composing.

Your body will never choose loss
So instead of focusing on how much less you want
Weight, fights, debt, worry
Focus on what more you want
Strength, harmony, freedom, certainty
It is in building the new that we are freed
Not in damning the old

Build it, and it will come
Empty out a drawer for someone
They will fill it
Share your work every day
People will find it
Walk and your legs will strengthen
Open your hours and your days will fill
Speak as though you've arrived
And reality will realign

There is no such thing as being idle
Even in rest the body is purging, storing, restoring
Letting the mind go quiet is not stepping into nothingness
It is allowing clarity and grace
It is replacing chaos with light

There is something you can learn from everyone. Anything you can learn, any book you can read or any song you can hear first came from the mind of another human being. And once you realize that all we ever really learn, receive, and experience comes from other human minds and hearts, you will never feel greater or less than another. You will only acknowledge that everyone has a different medicine, and our job is to find it and then share it with the world.

The path, like lines of a fingerprint, is unique to each of us
And so because there are no two lives alike
There is no need to compete with someone for your destiny
Abundance is everyone's fate

I learned to start moving with the moon
Obeying the trines
Resting when the stars were squaring
And moving when they were aligned
I used to laugh at people who believed in this
Until I came to find
The Earth is water like our bodies
And the moon controls the tides
The ecosystem we generated from
Was not an earthly body in its prime
It was stars and planets and solar systems
That are now cells of mine

When you heal yourself
You heal everyone
When you're reaping a harvest
You can feed everyone
Don't let anyone tell you
That taking care of yourself is selfish
It's the only path
To enlightening the whole

Give to everyone else
What you wish the world would give to you
You'd be astounded how much more satisfying
It is to offer
Than it is to demand
And to take

Everything exists in layers and iterations
Reality is a series of fragmented perspectives
No two are the same
The way the truth seems self-evident to you
As it does to someone else who has walked a different path
When you realize this
You will discover what it means to be at peace with others
And why so many of us aren't

And what will you do
With your wild, untethered days
Other than sit around pacifying
In the chains of expectation?

Real change happens in subtle motions
But mostly it's deciding to create a life
That didn't exist before
And that is the beauty of the things that break you
They force you to create yourself anew to move on
And perhaps that was the point
All along

Do you know how hard it is to liberate yourself
to be who you are

Do you know how much work it takes to believe

The space your body takes up is the amount of
Earth you get to hold

And your desire to be smaller, smaller, smaller

Comes from the belief that to be insignificant,
unbothersome

Is to be good?

There is a sort of magic on the other side of becoming
That doesn't seem to exist in just being
I imagine the monks would laugh at me
And say, child, becoming is just learning how to be

Imagine how things would feel
If you didn't know how they looked

Does your relationship improve
The more you are together

Or do you each deteriorate
Two misfit pieces
Grating against one another
Picking apart your contours
To fit with something
You were never meant for?

The closer you grow
The more finely your jagged edges
Should hug one another
As though they are not
Faults in your character
But spaces that mark you
As the one they've
Been waiting for
All this time

Because you don't recognize your soul mate
By the color of their hair
Or how certain you are that you've found them
So many people are so sure
And end up so wrong

You recognize them by flow
You recognize them because you vent to them

Not about them You recognize them because

you don't have to question
"Should we be together?"
You are too busy
Being

You recognize them because
They make you feel like love is no longer something
You need to take a break from
But what you can fall back onto
When the rest of the world is too much

The first night I chose sleep over him
Was the first I truly loved myself

Sometimes relationships end with you being confused

And that's their ending—confusion

Sometimes you fight for years only to discover

You were on the wrong side

One day you and your ex spoke for the last time

One day your mom picked you up for the last time

The saddest endings are the ones you don't realize are happening

The ones that don't end with a goodbye

The things that simply cease to exist

With no explanation—

No warning

There are no deadlines for your life
You don't have to pull the magic out of you
By some particular point in time
It is never too late for a miracle
The right time for anything to happen is now

The only prayer I have left
Is that I may do something today
That changes tomorrow

Love is not a sensation you transmute
It is something that someone's presence
Allows you to feel
As though their being
Gives your body permission
To release hormones
And heat
And hope

Which is why we fall just as much in love
With things that are not love
And people who are not loving
And why we want the perfect match
The one who makes our endocrine systems
Fire off without interruption

But I have to wonder
Why people crave so deeply
A feeling that's generated within them
A feeling that their body makes for itself

And why they wait to feel
What they're already capable of
If only they'd let it

When I began to break open
A symptom was random recollections

I began to remember
Recurring dreams I had years ago
Hallways in preschool
Things buried so deep
Only some divine awakening
Could unearth them in my mind

I stayed in a cabin one summer
In it, I baked a Fourth of July cake
And tried to write a book
But it was too hot when the icing went on
And I didn't have the ability
To write for thousands of words

But there I was
The little pieces of me
The things I would become
The things I would still love

They'd grow and they'd evolve and they'd become
At its core my whole life blossomed from seeds within me
I spent my years scavenging for them
But all I had to do was water them and give them light
What was already within me
Would inevitably grow
My job was not to plant them
But to make sure I was well enough
To let them take root

Three things are certain:
We are born
We die
We grow

Bodies mature, age, shed layers
Build new cells
You're creating CO_2 as you breathe
You're creating thoughts as you read this
The universe is expanding by the second
Oceans are chipping away at shorelines
Cities are ascending and expanding
And so are we
Growth is our homeostasis
And everything is done for its purpose

Your nature is not stasis

It is movement

The Earth does not look at itself and say,

"I am perfect, I am done,"

Nature's objective is not to complete

But to re-become

Again, and again

The tools of creation are not always a 1,000-mile walk, or despair and divorce and drugs and eccentricities and nomadic journeys that you reference to make metaphors and draw patterns and existential points about the ins and outs of things. Sometimes they are routine, and simplicity, and cleanliness. An easy life is not a boring life; it is a life unshackled. It is a life freed. You do not need to generate chaos to make something of yourself. Maybe your path is not to run to the horizon, but to take everything you think you need to throw out, and sweat until it's made beautiful.

What are you going to do
When you finally move on
When this last thing that needs to be fixed is fixed
And the worry subsides
And the problem is over
Like the dozens that preceded it
What will you do next?
That's what you should be doing now

How do you use your pain?
The answer to that question is your path.

You are not waiting for a time when it is easier
You are becoming better at being content

We do not need to be more
More good, more special, more, more—
We only need to know that our lives are insignificant
And millions have died, carelessly, and unremembered
And the world owes us nothing
And in a few generations, we will, maybe, be reduced
To a name mentioned now and again
When our children's children speak of their ancestors

And as we carry on, anxious about proving our significance
The Earth's seasons swell with the scent of springtime
And waves buckle and crash and rescind to where they came
And animals cuddle with their mothers under the trees
And miles of dark forests retain their enigmatic mystery
And the specks of white fire in the sky burn on

As the lives and stories and emotions
Of the millions before us
Have dissolved with the day
We, too, will forget these hours
We, too, will recall moments
And this one, like the many thousands prior
Will probably be forgotten
Just like us
Just like all of it

We are nothingness
Bearing witness to magnificence
And that is our freedom

Your mind is fire
It can heat your house
Or burn it to the ground

All of this, and what I'd come to find
Is that healing was really just changing
How I did the most ordinary things

I don't buy much anymore
I used to walk in circles
Around department stores
And the curved edges of
Barstools
Searching
But it's all seemed to dissolve
Into a more filling hunger
One that reaches
For the familiar black cotton dress
And the food that's been sitting in the pantry
Because I've stopped preparing for someday
Stopped wandering endless circles
Trying to fill my empty spaces
With things

But this is what happens when survival is a given
And status becomes our new obsession
We conflate our needs and wants
No wonder we are all so anxious
Imagine believing you need so much to get by

It is not the unknown
But the past you are projecting
Into it

Usually the fate you fear most
Is the one you're imposing on yourself now

You're not afraid that it will happen
You're afraid you'll never get out

The only ambition I have left
Is to be at peace each day
Anything that doesn't facilitate that
Is just noise

I am awed at the way
My heart swells when I hear the songs
I listened to at my darkest, seediest times
As though something so irrefutably beautiful
Was being planted
I just didn't know it at the time

Happiness, I know now
Is just clean white sheets
And hot black coffee
And hope
And hope

It is not creating yourself
It is allowing yourself
Every ounce of potential
Is already inside of you

You cannot become
Anything you already aren't
And you don't long for anything
That isn't already part of you

Every dream
Every thing
You've ever wanted
Is dormant

Sometimes it is pain
And sometimes it is light
That brings it forward

I have burned my life down
To the only things that matter
Writing every day
Sleeping and sweating

If on my last day
I were to greet
The person I could have become
I hope I am happy to be who I am
And I hope that I love her anyway

I stand outside the wide painted cabin wicks
And I am in the belly of god
Maybe that's what divinity is—
The scent of the forest, or springtime when it rains
The things that man cannot manufacture
That evoke the most guttural response in me
As though there's something in my cells
That recognizes their home

The way your conscious mind
Is a tiny fraction
Of the knowledge your body holds

The world you see
Is a thin veil
In front of a whole universe

Like how the bacteria in your gut
Responds to the knowledge you can't remember

When gusts of wind make you nostalgic
And synchronicity seems intentional
And you're awed by the familiar scent of spring
And grace guides you

The whole universe
Is reminding you
Of what, somewhere,
You already know

When you're feeling most helpless
It's comforting to ask for grace
But praying for it
Makes you believe it's something outside of you
Something you're waiting to be given

When you're feeling most helpless
You forget to wonder
What it does for someone else
To convince you
That your power can be redeemed
If only you follow their rules

This

    is

        just

            a hologram

Your ego
is your avatar

Your mind is
your control panel

The trick is not letting your ego believe
That one impermanent emotion
Can shield you from its opposite

That trickling anxiety thoughts
Throughout the day
Will vaccinate you from a panic attack

Allowing your darkness
Makes it as beautiful as your light

We need sages and scientists to expand the human mind
And we need to intersect grace and reason

How do you know that we all see the same colors
And don't just call them different thing
There is nothing as mysterious as another person's mind

Is it a problem
Or is it a distraction

Does it hold you back
Or do you use it to shield yourself
From what you actually fear?

I've read that the breath is the mind's remote control

Which is why they tell you do it deeply when you
need to relax

And vigorously when you're giving birth

And with power when you swing a punch

It is not a coincidence that you disrupt it when you're scared

And hold it when you're anxious

And just notice it when you meditate—not force it

Just realize that all of this power exists

Healing is not fixing
It is just the process of remembering
That everything was always okay

Evolution is divinity at work
We are nature made aware of itself
Science is the most spiritual pursuit
To learn the patchwork of existence
Is to understand ourselves

Your soul mate is the person
Who helps you build a home
Not the one who instantly feels like home

For home can be confused with comfort
And comfort is what we're used to
Which is why so many people
Assume forevers in the wrong arms

And confuse feeling for fate
Familiarity for family
Desire for love

Pain is often a signal that you have ceased
creating in your life

Something is dying and you're not putting
anything in its place

A signal that you're not paying attention

A signal that there's something you need to do

Like a hand on a hot stove

You are keeping yourself in danger

There is safety you are not moving to

We are taught
To fall in love with the time
That our lives leave us
In solitude

But what happens when
We become too good at aloneness
And too comfortable that we forget
We need other people?

Because the axing of vulnerability
Can dissolve the lingering pangs of loneliness
And being in control can begin to feel romantic
And we should love ourselves first, of course

But we were built in separation
To rekindle in togetherness
And we mustn't forget
That solitude prepares us for this
It is not our final destination

I once read that lonely people
Take hot baths more often
That it's like being connected to the womb

We need other people—
Which is perhaps the scariest
And most beautiful part of being alive

Sometimes we think money
Or work or beauty or accomplishment
Can do the job just as well

But human love is not of this world
So nothing in it can replace it

The strange burden of being an intuitive
In a world that's still asleep

Is that to be so sensitive that you can perceive what's wrong
Makes you feel like everything is yours to fix

What if you pretended
You were a character of your own design
And you were your own god
And you could hand yourself mercy
And you could change things yourself?
Who would you be?
And what would you do?

The strange burden of worrying

Is that you assume when you stop

All your worst fears will come true

As though premeditating horrors prevents them

As though living in stress and pain makes you better able to respond

As though you can beat fear to the finish line

Nothing in the universe is broken without reason
Nature doesn't work that way
Stars collapse and become supernovas
Seasons cycle to purge and renew
Your life will not break you without purpose
If you are opening to your rebirth
This is the crucifixion before you resurrect

The scientists say
You can speak to your cells
That your DNA doesn't unfold
It is controlled
And that it is listening
Even when you don't realize
Life is not happening to you
It is unfolding from you

In churches
They make you pray for forgiveness
Mercy
Strength

As though someone outside of you has them
As though god is someone you must beg
As though god is someone who wants to be worshipped

I don't trust a god
Who needs to be worshipped to grant salvation

That sounds a lot like
The kind of boyfriends my mom warned me about

I don't trust a god
Who makes you pray for courage
Because the things you're begging him for
Are already inside you

It makes you wonder:
Who wants to convince you they aren't?

I used to think heaven was
When I reverted back to perfect

And now I hope
It is swinging in a field

Staring at my chubby toes
And feeling the roll of my stomach
And letting knotted, grown-out roots lie by my sides
And a coffee stain reside
On the front of my dress

And it all being okay
And it all being beautiful

You are not improving your self

You are adjusting your world

To fit your self

You are getting used to being here

The opposite of love is not loss
It is obsession
We have a terrible time letting go
Of the things that make us feel

Pain is leftover impact
Reverberating between your molecules

Unless you let it echo back out to where it came
It will boomerang between your cells

Making you believe it's part of you
Making you believe it's part of now

Peace rests in
Beams of light across the foot of my bed in the afternoon
The illuminating of whatever is
Plans of what's possible
Maps of what's doable
Knowing that everything is figure-out-able—

The real love of a few
The kind of confidence that feels no need
To convince others of greatness

Simplicity
And all the beautiful messes
That scatter around the cleanliness

Because the order is not the meaning
It is the routinizing of survival
That parts the sea to thrive

I am pretty sure

The spotlight complex is a real epidemic

And I wonder

Why we never Google self-awareness

Because I can tell you

That my stressors are almost always not what's happening

But what I assume other people

Will assume of what's happening

And I can tell you

That if I didn't think I was being watched—
documented, daily

I would dress for the weather

And eat without guilt

And spend more afternoons

Marveling at the sky

Because things have become more about building a
digital legacy to outlast us

Than they are about building an existence for us, now

As though a constellation of pixels could recreate
the sensation

Of staring at the sky and feeling lightness course
through you

As though what we make other people feel

Is the same as what we do

I'd like to spend my time here

Playing with the stream of creation

That trickles out my fingers each day

The ideas that have come through

For days, for months, for years

Span beyond my finite mind

And I'd like to feel so humbled

When I consider the centuries of people who have lived
in these houses

And cooked on these stoves

And walked these streets to home

And how four walls create a world in itself

And how what's fated and what's manifested interweave

I am whatever I tell myself I am

My thoughts about myself are entropic
Without being stopped
Their energy circles, carries on
It keeps informing me
Of things that are no longer true

What a liberation
To realize this was the case
All along

The easier it is to lose
The harder it is to love

I quieted my life
Until the only thing I could hear
Was the sound that blood makes in your body
When you're still enough and listen
And the tapping of rain on the windowsill
And the simmer of sage leaves as they coil
The familiar clicking of a keyboard
And the steeliness of a frigid afternoon
Each of these an encryption
Reminding me what matters
Telling me where to go

Anything you can't get over
Is at its root a subtle addiction
A compulsion so quiet
It tricks you into thinking
You want it or you need it

It makes you think it's part of you
"I'm anxious," you say
"I am an anxious person"

That's what they say about abusive things—
Victims are first just people convinced
That they want the thing that breaks them

I am starting to think
That love has a half-life
Energy, after all, is a physical thing
It is not over when they leave
It ends when you
Burn, cry, write, sweat it out
Until what you shared is
Made manifest
You cannot throw it away

A miracle
Is not a rare intervention
It is a restoration of perception
It's not awe-inducing
It's commonplace
The only problem is
When you think it's not

They say there are 100 billion neurons
In every human brain
Only 15% are activated

That means there are more connections in your head
Than there are stars in the galaxy
Or people on Earth

There is a universe in your mind
A network of information to which
You rarely—if ever—access

Unclasp your hands
Nobody is coming to save you

And that is as it should be
Your whole life has been about finding
That you're meant to save yourself

Everything is just an avenue
To show you your own power

When I first got sick
I let go of the little things
I thought I didn't have energy for

Routines, walking, eating three meals

There was only one thing to do
And it was survive
What I didn't realize
Was that the walking, the eating,
The washing, the routines
They were the healing

And letting them go
Was the breaking

No person is just one person
We all exist in versions and iterations
Layers that are revealed
As a thousand perfect storms
Grow you, and change you, and show you
To you

The work of falling in love
Is not making two best selves gel
But in meeting all of someone's parts
And seeing whether or not
There's some fraction of yourself
That can understand them, too

The study says
Most people given placebos
Respond to them the same
As those given antidepressants
With the small exception
Of those who are most sick

Which makes me wonder
Why we've all gotten it in our heads
That we must suffer in the worst ways
And that we are helpless
When just believing that we are being fixed
Fixes us

And it makes me wonder
When we'll realize that god
And marriage and love and success
Are all just little pills that soothe us

We can be healed by ideas
That reveal not only the power they hold
But the power we do

What would happen if we realized
The magic was in how the neurons fire
And that we could choose the direction they shoot?

I wish I didn't know
What I weighed or
What other people's lives were like
I would be so blissfully ordinary
If these measures didn't exist

I do this to myself, I know
I let nice photos and résumé lines
Flowery ideas of how I think my life could be
Grow vines around the pain so thick
I can't even see through them

When I feel the heaviness come,
I say: *Look at all these beautiful things*
What have you to be sad about?
But the bones of the entire structure
Are just pain I've tried to hide

I hope you are always free enough
To become who you want to be
And you aren't stifled by the assumption
That you owe your younger self
A future that she would grow up
To discover she's outgrown

I am afraid of the thing that I want most,
Which is to be free
And to be free isn't uncommitted
To a love, to a person, to a town, to a job

It is just to know that
I am capable of anything
And I am ready for everything

What potential pains could I inflict
If I exercised my full capacity
And if I didn't premeditate every horror?
I cannot bear for an outside hell
To be worse than my inside one

When I was in middle school
I learned to suck in my stomach
I did this to avoid looking thicker
And I kept doing it, wearing tightly bound clothes
Until my permanent state was just holding

I let it out recently
I am a being in constant, oscillating movement
How did I not see then?
That I was suffocating my potential
So other people wouldn't be bothered?

Someone once told me
That there are poisons that taste like elixirs
And elixirs that taste like poisons

I hope that someday I'm not so naive to think
That one sip of a tonic will solve anything

I hope that someday I'm not compelled to take seriously
Things that claim to numb, or things that promise to fix

It was me!
It was me all along
I was the victim and I was the oppressor
My only disease was not seeing that
The disease is not seeing my power
I am the creator of my life
And I am what I create

Who would you be if you weren't afraid of anything?

You're not wrong because you aren't right for someone
You were mismatched
Not broken

I am leaving everything here today—
This, these words
This is my reckoning

You do not have to suffer

Your suffering doesn't make someone else's fair

Your suffering doesn't help

Suffering transforms you because it teaches you how not to suffer

Its purpose is to remove you from false illusion

Not to generate your worthiness for salvation

I am not sorry for the person I had to become
to heal myself from you

Go to the middle of the forest
And stay there for a while
At first your anxiety will be louder
With nothing left to distract you
But it will let you hear clearly
What your fear voice sounds like
And the more you commune with it
The less it will be able to convince you
That it's who you really are

If you can't lose those extra pounds

And you can't get him to commit

And the job keeps not working out

Maybe it's that it's not supposed to

And maybe your internal ecosystem is trying to
tell you something

Maybe you're choosing the wrong person

Maybe you're in the wrong field

Maybe the "no's" are the answers you're asking for

Maybe these rejections are outlining the path

I am whole because I see that
Rivers and tree trunks run in the same lines as my veins
When I look at my wrist up close
And I look at the world from afar

Everybody in your life is an assignment
And the project is not to fix them,
It's to change you

Be still
To meditate is not to stagnate
It is to step out of your own way
And let the constant stream of movement
Power through your being
It is to witness that this has been happening
The entire time

Let your life push you past the point of recovery
That is where we begin

Half the work of getting over anything
Is shining a light in the closet
And realizing there aren't any monsters inside

But what of the parts of you that aren't "I?"
Imagine laying all your organs on a table
You'd point to every one of them and say,
"My heart, my lungs, my eyes, my bones"
These are all the parts of you that aren't "I"
These are all the pieces of a form that belong to you

So when you feel too trapped in your body
Too weighed by potential harms
Start pointing to all that parts of you that aren't "I"
And remember that "I" is not in any of them
Because "I" is not of this Earth
And these earthly pains cannot touch "I,"
Even if they sever and disintegrate its parts

Over time, your body becomes your cage
Every time you confront pain, your fascia tightens
It makes it harder for you to repeat your actions
This is to keep you safe
But what happens when you've moved in every direction
And have been stung at every end?
This is when the cage becomes so restrictive
That just your breath starts cracking it
And that is the pain of awakening
You attribute it to something outside of you
But it's you breaking out of the comfort binds
That you think will save your life
They are the ones keeping you from life
In the first place

It's not that love won't save your life
It's that it can't
Love is a beautiful and important thing
But it cannot undo your chronic worrying
And it cannot forgive your past
It cannot decide who you should become
And it cannot push you to become it

My inspiration doesn't come from just sitting back and waiting

It comes from deliberately sorting through things, from creating other things

There's an engagement that life requires from us all

A presence that we can't fake or procrastinate into the void

When nowhere feels like home
It means you are being called to build one
When nothing feels okay
You are being called to ask why not
When you feel the most hopeless
You are being asked to rest
When you are certain you aren't beautiful enough
You are being asked to make beautiful the parts of you
You think it would be easier to change

Begging for a new life with your pain never works
Saying to god, "See how unfair this is?"
Is not how you get her to fix anything
And that's what you're doing with your pain
Calling for help with the work
That was always just yours

You can choose how you travel
You can decide where you're going
You will never know which route
Will be the one to take you there

So don't collapse when things
Don't seem to be working
Unanswered prayers are answers
Failed plans are signs
Even things that don't work out
Are still part of the path

Failures are detours
Not destinations

A coincidence is a sign
Serendipity is not an accident

Every emotion has a message
Every feeling has a purpose
Fear means you've determined that you love
Anxiety means you're too far into the past or future
Anger means you've recognized some form of truth—
Or identified how something should be different
Discomfort means something is not right,
And you're being offered the opportunity
To change it

I'm always having to remind myself
It is okay to be hungry
It is okay to rest
It is okay to do nothing but laugh in a day

There are no happy endings
There are, at best, happy days
Happy moments
And they do not come because
The world has stopped being broken
And handing you hardship
They come because you've learned
You've learned how to respond
You've learned how to become
And you know what to do now
Self-reliance is peace

Conventional wisdom tells us to trust our feelings. Spirituality often seems to imply that our emotions are earpieces to the universe, that using our instincts, which are connected to our subconscious minds—the roughly 90% of information that our brains don't retain conscious knowledge of—we can predict, or "just know," what's going to happen. There's good reason for this. There's a lot of research that tells us we can benefit tremendously from being tuned into ourselves. But this advice is not foolproof. We're often only hearing half the story.

We should not trust everything we feel. Not every single thing we feel is true or means something about what will be true. We frequently confuse a fear for an "instinct" or trust a feeling that's based on an irrational thought as though it's one that's based in reality. In fact, learning to override some of our strongest, most compelling emotions is how we find healing, achievement, health, and enlightenment. The issue is not that we need to feel less, but that we need to be able to interpret how we feel with conscious, critical logic. Our emotional navigation systems only work when we have a discerning mind in the driver's seat.

Sometimes the partners we have the strongest feelings for end up being the unhealthiest relationships for us—our attachments to them comfortable recreations of the relationships we knew in childhood. Sometimes the careers we think we will love doing are the ones we are least suited for, but blinded by passion, we burn away our years chasing them. Sometimes our procrastination is not an indication that we're "on the wrong path"; rather, that we're just being lazy or don't know how to act in spite of meaningless discomforts. Sometimes avoiding a situation is not what's healthiest for us emotionally, and exposing ourselves to it would liberate us for good. Sometimes a relationship isn't "meant to be," no matter how strongly we feel otherwise. Sometimes we dissolve relationships that were actually very good for us due to common frustrations that were never woven into our "fairy tale love" narrative—and so we assume they are markers of it being "wrong."

Emotions cannot give us the answers to these dilemmas. Misunderstood emotions create these dilemmas.

If you don't have what you want right now
You are being prepared for what you want
And that is usually the problem
Everyone eventually gets
Exactly what they want

I wish I had a name for the hunger in me
The kind that nothing seems to feed
I wish I could water out the fires in me
So all that's left of them is steam

Maybe you keep creating problems
Because it means you can express and witness
Your inner power
Maybe you are not addicted to the darkness
But in playing with your light

Passion is the spark that lights the fire
Purpose is the kindling that keeps it burning all night
Your passion is the fleeting emotion

You cannot build a life on sparks that last seconds
But the embers they leave, the slower fuel
That is the gold mine

Your future is dormant within you

Did Jesus leave the lepers
Because he didn't like their "vibes?"
When did we start thinking love
Was an intolerance of negativity?
When it's being able to stand within it
And not be influenced
Patching the holes in the bottom of your ship
So whether you're in a shallow stream
Or miles deep in the ocean
You can still float
You can still be

I don't know why this is

I don't know why the universe is constantly expanding,

Or why nature is evolving and then
destroying itself only to begin again

I imagine the answer is too complex for a human mind
to understand,

But I also imagine that if we could know

It would be so simple and beautiful, it would move us
to tears

Something like: Matter is conscious and
it's so in love with its potential

It just wants to see everything it can do

Your whole life is not a journey of creating yourself,
But witnessing that you are already complete
A shedding of illusion

The value is in the room
Each moment is pure potential
You either let your mind
Keep recreating what it's known,
Or you start playing with the light

Your doings are binding
Your mind is adapting as you
Do, as you say, as you think

What a searing truth

That every sour love I've chosen

Has unveiled some part of me

I tried to keep secret

Some part that was strong enough

To silently choose the person

Who could bend my ego far enough back

And let her free

Your emotions are not your energy
They are responding to your energy
It's like confusing the weather
With the entire universe

All of this unexplainable suffering
Is knowing something is wrong
Without knowing what the alternative would be
And how is that?
That we can know what's wrong
And not realize it's an extrasensory perception
Being in a reality in which it's right
That life dripping down into this one
Telling us:
Here is the way out

And do you know that what they say about you
Is what they really fear about themselves?

I exist in the midst of infinite abundance

I myself am infinite potential

Witnessing my dreams come true is my destiny

Holding the abundance of the Earth is my fate

I say thank you for my unanswered prayers

They were portals to my miracles

I say thank you for the challenges in my way

They are redirects to my path

I command the godhead within to release every cell

From patterning, threads of karma, illness, pain

I open my immaterial eye

To recognize the potential today will offer me

To change my life forever

I ask myself now

What I can do today to move closer

To the person I want and am meant to be?

You want to know when you're wasting your life?

When you check your phone though there's no notification

But you refresh, refresh—trying to find one

When you scroll to pass time

Because there is something uncomfortable in the moment

Begging you to change it

When you don't know what you want next

Because you haven't been able to sit
with yourself long enough to ask

Who am I becoming?

When you fear the future more than you are excited for it

Because you have placed your faith

In what the world will give you

Rather than what you will create

Sometimes the only purpose someone has in our lives
Is to make us feel something we didn't know was in us

Maybe you were the hero you were waiting for

Maybe you were the love of your life all along

Maybe you were always happy

And just thought you needed the reassurance of someone safe

To let yourself feel it

It is all a swinging pendulum
A hard hit back only means
You're being prepared to move forward
And each time you do
You're in a newer world than before
You never go back to where you started
That place doesn't exist
And neither does the old you

Do you know what happens when you light a fire within you?
It burns everything that's standing in the way

Being truly fulfilled
Is an impenetrable shield
There is no resistance to an insult
There is no need for someone to approve
There exists such a deep joy
And nobody else's words put it there
So nobody else's words can take it away

A microcosm of cells and stars
Expanding inversely
If only the microscopes could see
The mini-universes our atoms
Are the planets of

Every day, you make your last memory
With every person you see
But people don't stagnate
Even after our ideas of them stop forming
Give people a chance to show you who they've become
Give them the space to change
And then believe them the first time
When they show you how much they have
Or how much they've stayed the same

Wait for the reckoning
There is always a reckoning

The things you lose are not lost
They are part of you, they have built you
Their job is finished
What's no longer in front of you
Is now within you
The things that linger
Are still at work

Nature echoes what humans resist
That cocoons burst open
And stars implode into supernovas
And that birth is painful to the one delivering
And that to become who we are
We must shed who we aren't
We must allow ourselves the storm

The question is always:
If this thought, if this choice, if this feeling
Isn't serving me,
Then whom am I sustaining it for?
To whom am I offering my life force?
And to what am I handing my power?

Sometimes you will go through darkness,
And that is the end of the sentence
It was a dark winter, and nothing more
You sank and you purged
And you didn't understand why you laid in sadness
Sometimes you don't need to know why
You only need to go through it

Your life is an echo

Everything is feedback

If you want to know how you're doing

Look at how the world is responding

Reading has shaped me, unshaped me,
bothered me, and taught me

I healed because I learned to think as other people wrote

Live so that death has nothing to steal

I seared my fractured lines with possibility
I am not healed because I am whole
I am healed because I adapt now

When I was a little girl
I remember standing
Letting waves run over my scrapes

Mama said salt water heals

And everything that pours
From your body's releasing
Is salt water

And everything that heals creates salt water
And everything that breaks us makes salt water

BRIANNA WIEST is a writer, author, and editor. She has published thousands of articles that have been read by millions of people throughout the world. She currently works for a variety of national publications. This is her fourth book published by Thought Catalog Books.

For more information, or to book Brianna for writing or speaking engagements, please visit *briannawiest.com*.

MORE FROM
BRIANNA WIEST

101 Essays That Will Change The Way You Think

I Am The Hero Of My Own Life

The Mountain Is You

Ceremony

THOUGHT
CATALOG
Books

BROOKLYN, NY